Up the Ancient Pathway

A Children's Book for All Ages

"The people who walked in darkness have seen a great light; Those who dwelt in the land of the shadow of death, upon them a light has shined." Isaiah 9:2 NKJV

MICHAELA COZAD

"Thus says the Lord, 'Stand by the roads and look; ask for the ancient paths, Where the good way is, then walk in it, And you will find rest for your souls.'" Jeremiah 6:16 AMP

"'Why all this grief and weeping? Don't you know the *[children] are not dead, but merely asleep?'" Mark 5:39 TPT

I will start this story by telling you a secret: she was a diamond.

Though she did not know it, she was indeed a Diamond among Rubies, Emeralds, and Sapphires. Just a child, she found wonder and beauty in all things. Her name was Prism.

Prism lived in the Kingdom of Celestia, near a small town called Slumber. Slumber was a quaint village, nestled in a deep valley surrounded by two large mountains.

Fog from the mountains would roll down and settle onto the village, creating a quiet and comfortable place for the people to stay. So comfortable in fact, that time seemed to move slowly, and the people there lived their lives half-asleep.

The people of Slumber were known as the "Jeweled Ones." Clothed in rich colors and precious stones, the Jeweled Ones prided themselves in their important duties and status within the town. Each villager of Slumber belonged to a clan: Rubies, Sapphires, and Emeralds, and the color of your stone meant you were accepted. Everything in this sleepy little town revolved around the color of your stone, and where you belonged.

But Prism was not a native of Slumber. Her stone was neither Ruby, Sapphire, or Emerald, but clear. It wasn't cut and polished like the stones of the other clans, but rough and irregular. Her clothes weren't rich in color, or adorned with special threads either. She only wore a simple white dress that flowed as freely as her wild hair and spirit. She was different, and struggled to fit in the sleepy culture around her.

Nonetheless, Prism would wake up, and tenderly hold her clear, rough stone in her hands, and say to herself "Perhaps today someone will see something special about my little stone. It must be special somehow."

Then with a smile, she would tuck the stone back under the safety of her collar, close to her chest, and walk into town with a hope that she would find her place in the world.

As Prism walked along, she noticed a small break in the fog, where a patch of pure sunlight broke through. The ground where the sun hit sparkled and appeared alive, and Prism noticed there was a small, narrow path, that wound into the forest and up the mountain.

"Do I dare?" Prism asked aloud to herself. "Should I leave the comfort of this hazy valley?" She glanced around her. "The path looks ancient, and like it hasn't seen anyone for ages… The Jeweled Ones warn of such paths, that they lead children astray into the woods, and that they become lost forever…" Prism started slowly up the narrow path into the trees, and though her mind was hesitant, her heart was curious and compelled.

Prism walked further up the mountain, and deeper into the forest. She didn't realize how far she'd gone until she broke out of the fog, and could see the whole town of Slumber in the valley below. "It looks so small from up here…" she whispered to herself.

Compelled by a sensation she couldn't quite recognize, but what could only be described as the blurriness of distant memories, she passed through a gate into a small clearing. The soft dewy grass, plush on her feet, was speckled with a plethora of wild flowers. A bubbling stream weaved through the surrounding trees into a small pool. And in the center, under the warmth of the direct rays of sun, glistened a large flat stone. "There's a peace, yet mystery, about this place…" thought the young girl. She sat herself upon the rock, and closed her eyes, soaking in the freshness of the air and the warming rays of sun.

Breathing deep and connecting to the beauty of the world around her, Prism found a place beyond Slumber, and for the first time found rest.

Daily Prism would find herself coming back to this place, up the forgotten ancient path, either on her way in or out of town. Sometimes she would visit multiple times a day. There was something familiar about the way the place made her feel. There, on the rock, she was safe. It didn't matter what color her stone was, or what she wore, or even that she was a child. Sometimes she would take her stone from behind her collar, and glance at it, and it would even look almost pretty in that sparkling sunlight. The more Prism visited her "secret garden," the more herself she felt, but the more different she felt in town. Slumber seemed grayer than it did before, and the townspeople sleepier than she ever realized. Still, there was a part of her that wondered why she was so different, and if anyone would ever accept the tiny treasure she kept close to her heart.

One morning, Prism was in her secret garden, contemplating these things, and tears started to roll down her cheeks. The presence was heavier that day, and she could hardly contain the sweetness of it all.

"Welcome back, my friend..." called a voice.

Prism wiped the tears away and opened her eyes. A being, a young girl appearing not much older than herself, emerged from the water. Her dress was as sheer as the water itself, and her flowing hair was adorned with flowers. She moved both slowly and sweetly, but there was a certain wildness in her eyes.

Who are you?" Prism asked.

"I go by many names," the young being responded, "Teacher, Comforter,

Encourager, Spirit of Divinity, Friend." The being chuckled, shaking water and flowers from her hair, and said "but you can call me Brooke, for I come from this spring of living water. Welcome to the Garden of the Ancient Ones, Prism."

Prism was surprised. "How do you know my name?" she asked.

"I am the Spirit of the Great King Divine, who knows, sees, and rules over all of Celestia. He sent me here to you, to reveal who you are and where you belong."

Prism was both excited and troubled by this. Prism greatly loved the Great King, and His kind Son. She had known of Him since she was a little girl, and the Sapphires taught of His wonderful miracles and sacrifices. But could He actually help her change the color of her stone?

"That may prove difficult, even for Him," she stated as she pulled out her stone. "See, everyone in the town of Slumber belongs to a clan, and each clan does important things for the town. Your clan is identified by the color of your stone, but my stone has no color. The people think I am strange, and I do not belong anywhere."

"Here," Brooke the Spirit replied as she pulled out a mirror from among the stones in the water. "This mirror is made from living stones, shaped by the waters of the stream. Gaze into it and you will see the truth of who you are, and find a most precious treasure."

Prism carefully held the mirror, curious about what she would find in its face, but the only thing she saw when she gazed into it was her own reflection.

"I don't see anything." She said confused.

"Look closely, and the answer will come." Brooke replied, as she slowly vanished back into the pool of water.

Prism started back down the mountain and into town, with the mirror in her pocket and her stone next to her chest. She pondered the words of Brooke in her heart, and wondered what could all these things mean? The Garden of the Ancient Ones, a mirror that could show her a treasure and give her a place to belong, and a Great King that can see all, it was all so much to contain. She glanced into the delicate mirror as she walked the wide path back into town, but again all she could see was her own face. "How curious..." She whispered to herself.

As the child entered into town, she noticed that the fog over Slumber was denser than before. The air was heavy, but not in the sweet way the presence of Brooke created. It was heavy in a way that felt that all the weight was resting on her shoulders. She noticed it was harder to both breathe and see.

"Isn't it such a beautiful day?" She heard one Emerald say to another in passing.

"Yes," replied the other, "I just love the fresh air."

"This is not fresh air…" Prism thought to herself, shaking her head.

Prism entered the town square, hoping to find someone who could help her decipher what she was supposed to see in the magic mirror. "I shall go to the clan leader of the Rubies," she said to herself, "they are wise in justice and rule over the order of Slumber. Surely they will be able to see the truth in this mirror."

She entered the home of the Ruby clan. A great marble structure, with three pillars at its entrance. Prism walked into a large room with many of the Rubies sleeping over their books and papers, mumbling and arguing nonsenses.

"I am looking for the leader of the clan of Rubies." Prism called out. "I am hoping you can help me see the truth hidden within this magic mirror, so I may find where I belong." She held out the mirror, but no one moved.

"Hellooooo!," she called out again.

A large figure, dressed in a velvet robe of deep red, started to stir. Seated on a large marble pedestal, he held a gavel in his hand. He slowly blinked, and lifted his large wobbly head, and through half opened eyes looked for the voice that called out.

"Who is there?" his voice boomed.

"I am Prism," the child replied. "I am looking for the Ruby clan leader. I need help seeing the truth in this magic mirror, it is supposed to reveal a great treasure and show me where I belong." Prism held up the mirror.

"I am Law," replied the man, "and I am the leader of the Ruby clan. Let me see this mirror you speak of."

He took the mirror and gazed into its face. "Ah!" he bolstered. "The answer is clear!"

Prism smiled, excited to know what the Ruby Leader saw.

"I see my crown, and my beautiful ruby stone," replied Law, admiring his reflection in the mirror.

"What do you mean?" Prism asked.

"This large golden crown on my head represents Government, and this ruby gives me authority over

Government. Only by abiding the law is truth found. Laws, orders, rules, are the true treasure you seek." He handed back the mirror. Prism took it and looked, but neither saw rubies, nor laws, nor rules.

"I don't understand." She said softly.

"Of course not," replied Law, "you are but a child, and not a Ruby. You don't belong in the office of Government."

And with that the Ruby Leader nodded back into a lull, his eyes glazed over and almost completely shut, leaving Prism to her own thoughts.

Prism left the Ruby clan more confused than before. "Surely this can't be the truth Brooke spoke of, for I do not see rubies or laws, but only my own reflection." She looked up to see a Sapphire, a priest, who teaches the people about the Great King Divine.

"A Sapphire, he must know what truths lie in this mirror!" Prism exclaimed. "For he speaks to the Great King Divine himself!"

"Excuse me," Prism called out as she approached the Sapphire, who languidly walked out of a chapel mumbling important prayers. "My name is Prism, and I am trying to find the truths hidden within this magic mirror." She handed it to the Sapphire priest, who was now rustled from his docile state. "It's supposed to reveal a precious treasure and help me find where I belong."

The Sapphire priest responded, "I am Doctrine, leader of the Sapphire clan. I will share with you the truths you seek."

Doctrine carefully inspected the mirror. "Where did you get this?," he inquired.

"From a small pool at the end of a stream," Prism replied, "up an ancient pathway that leads into the mountains."

The Sapphire priest gently rubbed his chin. "I have heard of such paths. It is said that they were the paths our ancestors used to travel down the mountain in order to settle into this valley." Doctrine smiled fondly. His eyes even appeared more alive as he spoke.

Prism listened intently, but as soon as the Sapphire Priest's story started, it ended. Doctrine shook his head, as if trying to pull himself back to the moment, and rebutted. "Such pathways are irrelevant to us now. They were only for that time, for now we have settled well into this comfortable valley, and know all the laws and customs required in order to speak to the Great King. I would recommend not taking such unusual pathways, especially for a young child. To do so now is both folly and dangerous."

"Now let us see what truths this mirror holds." Doctrine looked deep into the face of the mirror. "Yes, indeed..." He said nodding as he handed it back to the girl. "What did you see?" She asked.

"I saw my blue satin cloak and hood, with my sapphire stone." He answered, returning to his drowsy state.

"Your what?" She asked confused, looking into the mirror and then back up at the Sapphire priest.

"This cloak and hood means I am a holy man, and this sapphire gives me the authority to talk to the Great King Divine." Doctrine explained. "Dear child, truth is found in our service to the King. Acts of devotion and piety, and practicing great prayers are the ways to truly please Him."

Prism was doubtful, for she did not see any sapphires or cloaks or special prayers in the mirror. However, she was sure that Doctrine must be right, because he spoke to the Great King, and this mirror was a gift from Him.

"How do I serve and talk with the Great King Divine?" She asked the Sapphire priest.

Doctrine chuckled as he yawned, and patted her on the head.

"Dear girl," he explained, "you are just a child. Only Sapphires know how to truly serve and can speak to the King, and you must learn under a Sapphire for many years. Do not worry, though, for I will speak to the Great King Divine for you."

And with that, Doctrine lulled back into his practice, mumbling his prayers, and returned to his sleep-walking.

Prism now felt more dejected than ever. Though she loved the Great King and His Son, she couldn't even serve Him. "What a miserable wretch I am," she said to herself as she started to walk back home.

"Don't listen to those pompous snakes in government and piety."

Prism looked up to see a tall woman, dressed in green.

"An Emerald!" Prism thought.

"Rubies and Sapphires think they're so great," spoke the Emerald woman, rolling her eyes. "They deceive themselves of their selfish desire for self-importance by masking it as a great service to the people of Slumber."

The Emerald woman's voice was as silky as her long green dress, but had a venom to it that made Prism afraid to speak.

"I couldn't help by overhearing…" The woman continued as she sauntered over to the girl. "My name is Avarice, and I am the leader of the Emerald clan." She tenderly placed one hand on Prism's shoulder, while the other seamlessly took the mirror out of her hands. "And I don't even need to look into this mirror to tell you its truths, dear."

Prism looked up into Avarice's face. It was beautiful, but her eyes were sinister. "What do you mean?" the child asked.

Avarice swung the mirror around as she explained. "Wealth, darling, is the greatest treasure. Rubies and Sapphires only care about their positions, because that's where they get their power. But wealth…" She says pulling out a gold coin… "wealth can influence both law and persuade piety."

Avarice laughed to herself. "Law thinks he can govern people and establish order with his rules. Doctrine thinks his practices can connect people to the Great King… But throw a little money their way and all those great philosophies of theirs change." She sighed and looked coyly at the girl. "We're all just trying to fit in and find our place of influence, using deceit and manipulation in order to get there. At least I am the only one who will admit it. And that, darling," Avarice said as she started to hand Prism back the mirror, "is the actual truth."

By this time, the sun was starting to set behind the mountains, and darkness was coming upon the town.

"I need to be going." Prism said slowly as she started to reach for her precious mirror.

"One more thing…" Avarice almost sang as she pulled back the mirror with a genteel flick of her wrist. "How about I take this wretched mirror off your hands? Though it's purpose is entirely useless, I'll even pay you for it."

"I don't want any gold." Prism replied.

"That's not what I was offering." Avarice responded as she pulled a dark, sparkly, green stone from her dress pocket. "I was thinking this." She extended the sparkling green emerald to Prism. The tantalizing shimmer captivated Prism's eyes, and Avarice sensed the temptation.

"Isn't this what you want?" Avarice continued, holding the stone up in what was left of the hazy sunset. "A real stone, a clan, a place to belong…"

Prism started to reach for the emerald.

"Yes, darling. You now know truth, and have a place of belonging, both which the mirror promised but never provided."

It was a delicious temptation, and Prism was within reach of all she desired, when the eyes of Brooke flashed in her memory. Those wild eyes were now a flame, and stared into the depths of her soul.

Prism quickly retracted her hand. "No! No thank you."

"Suit yourself," said Avarice dryly, handing back the mirror. "But I'll be waiting for when you change your mind."

Prism quickly grabbed the mirror and hurriedly ran out of town. As she ran, she started to cry. What felt like such hope that morning left her more confused and empty than ever. Prism started to think about her secret garden, and though the only thing her soul wanted to do was go home and cry, her heart longed for the serenity and peace she found in that place. But now the sun was well behind the mountains, and the whole valley was covered in night, and Prism's eyes were so strained and blurred from crying that seeing was nearly impossible. Just as it appeared all hope of finding her path was lost, Prism caught a glimpse of the shimmering ends of Brooke's hair reflected in the moonlight, as she ran into the woods.

"Brooke!" Prism cried out through her tears as she ran after her. "Spirit, wait!"

Prism ran as fast as her little legs could carry her, grappling and fighting branches and rocks and tears along her way through the dark forest. And though it was hard, and the journey felt more of a struggle than it ever felt before, Brooke, Spirit of the Great King Divine, would appear like a flash in the night, as if guiding her along the way.

At last, Prism burst out of the trees and into the clearing of her secret garden. The rock on which she sat numerous times still sparkled, even in the light of the moon. Exhausted, Prism laid over the rock and started to weep. "All I ever wanted was one thing." She cried between sobs. "I just wanted to belong."

"Did you find what you were looking for?"

Prism looked up to see Brooke standing upon the water.

"No," the child responded as she wiped her face. "There must be something wrong with me, because I can't see what the mirror is showing, and I asked all the important leaders in the valley of Slumber, and nothing makes sense now..." Prism tried to refrain from any more crying, but couldn't help a few sniffles.

"You haven't asked everyone," replied Brooke with a smile, "come with me."

Brooke extended her slender hand to the child. Prism stood to her feet, a bit unsure.

"Where are we going?" Prism asked.

"To go ask the Great King Divine." Brooke responded. "It is His mirror after all."

Prism's eyes went wide with fear, and she shook her head. "Oh no, I can't! I'm not a Sapphire."

"You don't have to be." Brooke replied.

Prism took Brooke by the hand, and was led to the edge of the pool.

"Now we jump." Brooke instructed. Prism's eyes lit with terror.

"Into the water?" She exclaimed. "What if I drown? What if I can't swim or find my way back?" Brooke laughed, but Prism could tell it was a different kind of laugh. When Avarice laughed, it felt empty and cynical, but Brooke's laugh gave Prism hope. Brooke looked at Prism with those wild eyes once more, full of mystery. "It's the only way," she said. "You must sink in order to elevate."

So in jumped the child and the Spirit, hand in hand. Prism found herself sinking slowly into the sweetest waters she ever tasted, and it was thick, like honey. There was an exhilaration that made her a little uneasy, but there wasn't fear. And the more she sank, the more she wanted to, for it felt like nothing she knew before. Yet it was familiar, like the feeling of coming home.

Slowly the light around her began to change, bursts of pure light like sparkles, but more and more brighter started to surround her. Prism felt that she was both sinking and being lifted into the light. She soon found herself coming up through the light, until she was seated, like she always sat upon her rock, but this time upon a large cloud. The air in this place was pure light, almost white, but warm. The cloud carried Prism through the light. It was so bright that Prism couldn't quite see anything, but she could hear and feel more than she ever did before.

"Ah, Spirit!" exclaimed a joyous voice. "Another daughter has found her way home!" Prism could hear the melodic laughter of Brooke. "I can't wait for her to meet Father," the voice continued, "He has missed her so."

"Daughter? Father?" Prism thought to herself.

Soon her eyes started to adjust to the light, and Prism found herself floating toward a monumental throne. She saw three figures, and it was from them which all the light was radiating from.

The first figure she recognized as Brooke. The Spirit was dancing and smiling, and was next to another figure. He had the stature and poise of a young man, but the eyes and expressions of a child. The two beings were obviously very close. The final figure Prism could barely observe. He was massive, all light, and the one seated on the throne. The cloud carrying the young girl floated and rested at the base of the throne. Prism knew she was in the presence of the Great King Divine, and she dared not look up.

"Father," the Young Man spoke, and though His voice was mature, Prism heard joy and youth in it, "this is the one Spirit and I have been telling you about."

"Ah, yes," said the Great King, His voice deep and resonating, but gentle. "Come, my child."

The Great King reached down, and picked up the cloud the child was

sitting on. As He lifted His hand towards His face, the cloud dissipated, and Prism was left snuggled perfectly in the palm of His hand.

"I've heard you've been on quite a journey." The Great King said.

The girl nodded. "My name is Prism," she began, "and Brooke, uhm I mean Spirit, gave me this mirror. It's from the pool of water at the end of an ancient path I found. I was there, searching I guess, for who I am and where I belong. It was there that She told me this mirror was from You, and that if I would only gaze into it, I would see a great treasure, truth, and know where I belong."

Prism began to cry softly as she relayed her story. The gentle King took the thumb of His other hand and wiped the child's tears. Prism glanced up at Him, and though she could not clearly see His face through the light and glory around Him, she could see His eyes. They were soft with wrinkles, not from age, but from wisdom, and kindness, and love.

"I know, dear one. I know it all, because I've been watching over you." He said.

"We all have," replied the Young Man.

"We were always there," added Spirit.

"What do you mean?" Prism asked.

"Pull out your stone.", the Great King instructed. Prism gently pulled out the stone from behind her collar. "And the mirror." The King added.

The young child held both of the most precious objects she ever owned in her two hands.

"Now look into the mirror, and you will find my greatest treasure."

Prism looked into the mirror, but once again, only saw her own reflection.

"I only see myself." said the girl sadly.

"Exactly," replied the Great King Divine, "you are my greatest treasure."

Prism, both shocked and little confused, gazed into the mirror again, and a beautiful story started to be revealed. Prism saw her little valley, full of light, and teeming with life. "There's no fog." She said.

"That is Bliss," explained the Great King, "Slumber is not its real name. When We created Bliss, it was meant as an oasis for my Sons and Daughters to live. The town only became Slumber after my Sons and Daughters allowed the fog to settle in."

Enamored, Prism focused back onto the mirror.

Prism watched as children, all dressed in white like herself, walk down the ancient pathway into the valley of Bliss. They were accompanied by the Young Man, who was the Great King's son. Birthed from the pool that Spirit had Prism jump into, the children would meet the Son with a tender embrace. Many called Him Savior, some called Him Wonderful, and others called Him Peace. He would talk and laugh with each child on their way down the mountain, and encourage them as each child walked the path into town. Some would come back up the pathway and jump in the pool to visit the Great King, His Son, and Spirit. However, more and more children didn't. They grew up and were no longer children, a fog started to settle over the valley, and the pathway was forgotten.

"It's so sad." Prism said softly. "But what does this have to do with me?"

"Let me see your stone," said the Great King. Prism held it up, and the Great King Divine took it gently and handed it to the Son. The Son carefully started to polish it with a scarlet cloth, and the Great King started to explain.

"All Jeweled Ones are my children. Born of the three of Us here in the Kingdom Realm of Celestia, they are birthed as spirit and take the journey down the mountain into flesh, so that they may take care of the world of Bliss that We all created.

However, darkness fell upon the valley, and the spirit within my children started to die. My children became separated from Us, and were starting to forget Us. So my Son walked down the path and into the valley to become flesh. The darkness tried, but could not overtake Him. He conquered the darkness through His life, His death, and His return to life, allowing the Light that radiates from Our being to shine once again onto the valley."

"I know this story." Said the young girl with awe. "The Sapphires teach it. If we choose to love the Great King and His Son, then the light will shine upon us."

"Yes," smiled the Great King, "but the Light was meant to do more. When you choose to love the Son, you are born again of the living waters of the Spirit Pool. Your inner spirit not only comes back to life, but you have access to My throne. My Son sacrificed Himself and taught these things, so that all my children may again walk the pathway and jump into the pool, so that they may speak and be one with Us. Some received, and have walked such pathways as you have. Others would not open their hearts to such things, and they traded their Diamonds from this realm for other stones in the valley. They allowed a fog to start hovering over them, until it became so thick that they eventually fell asleep."

"This is your stone." The Son said holding it up. "It is a Diamond, given from my Father Himself. It is clear and pure and innocent, like the love you have for Me and Father. It does not belong in the fancy garments found in the valley below, but is a part of your glory garments as a daughter, as a queen and a priest of Celestia."

The Son gently placed Prism's Diamond into the center of a delicate crown, surrounded by many other diamonds and precious stones.

Spirit, carefully took the crown and placed it on the child's head.

"Welcome home, Daughter!" all three Beings cried with joy.

Prism could not believe what was happening. It was all she ever wanted, and so much more. A stone, and a crown, and a family, all even more beautiful than those of the valley below her. She carefully took the delicate crown from her head, and caressed it ever so gently like she did before, back when it was just an uncut clear stone.

"What's the matter?" asked the Great King.

"Nothing," the child replied, "this is more than I even dreamed. But..." she gently placed the crown down in front of her, into the King's hand. "I don't need it. Everything I ever truly wanted is right here, with you, Father."

Suddenly, the Light of the three Beings intensified. The Light became so bright that it shined through the Diamond and through the young girl herself, and the whole realm was filled with beautiful rays and shapes of living color. Colors more rich than the reds, blues, and greens in Slumber, and colors that danced and breathed. It took Prism a short moment to realize that the Light of the three Beings was shining through her, creating rainbows.

"What does this mean?" She asked in awe.

"She has chosen the greater thing!" Exclaimed the Son with laughter and tears.

"Indeed, she has!" Chuckled the Father.

"All are born of Us," explained Spirit, "but few choose to be born of the Spirit Pool once more. Even fewer choose the greater thing. That is, walking the ancient pathway, communing with us, and allowing the Father to hold the crown."

"But who wouldn't want to sit here? Who wouldn't want to know the Father?" Cried the girl. "Who wouldn't choose this love?"

"It is because they fell asleep." Replied the Son with a sigh. "They can see and feel a little of the Light, but they are not awaken to its fullness."

"Yes…" added the Father, rubbing His chin with a twinkle in His eye. "If only someone would share the truth with those in the valley. If only someone would share the victory of My Son, the friendship of My Spirit, and the love of My Heart, so that they may awaken and clear out the fog. But who could be my messenger? Who could I send?"

Prism's eyes and arm shot up. "I will! I will go for you!"

The Father laughed a hearty, belly-full laugh. "Of course you will, my child!"

Spirit took the scarlet cloth from the Son, and touched Prism's lips, as the child began to weep with joy.

"I.. I remember…," cried the girl. Millions of memories started flashing through her mind, and the joy could only come out in tears. "I remember this place."

"I remember when you created the Blissful Valley. I was there when you painted the waters." Prism couldn't tell whether she was laughing or crying, whether she was rightside-up or down. "I remember walking the ancient pathway with the Son, I remember being seated upon Him, on the rock, in the secret garden. I remember the voice of Spirit comforting me as I cried. And I remember this, I remember agreeing to this… This moment now." Prism could not help but weep.

Spirit wrapped her arms around Prism, and comforted the child. Prism felt the tears of the Father fall upon her like warm milk and wine.

With kindness, he spoke. "Listen child, to the truths I am to share with you."

"All my children are Diamonds. They were made to carry my light, and let it shine through them, so that the color of their calling will shine into the valley. However, many of them chose the calling over Me, and created artificial stones. Let me explain.

Law represents my children who were created as ambassadors, to preside over the Government of my Kingdom. They are created to desire and reign with Justice, but have lost connection with my Justice. I gave them the law so that they may come to know their need for Me more. Only through Me can they understand the true purpose of Law, Order, and Justice. My Justice is fulfilled through the throne of My Son, the throne of Mercy. Law traded the color scarlet, the color of Mercy, for the lower color ruby."

"Doctrine represents my children who were created to teach about Me, about Us. They were gifted to lead others in worship and to shepherd the journey of coming to Me. However, in the fog, they traded truly knowing oneness with Us for knowing of Us. Their worship became ritual, and they wanted to hold the rituals for themselves, because it made them feel closer to Us than the other children. Truth is, they know very little of Us. They pick and choose my Words, and have become afraid to know My Spirit. They traded the blue hues of oneness with Spirit, for the lower sapphire color of knowing about spirit."

"Avarice represents all my other children, who lost touch with Me, and listened to the dark voices of fear, greed, and envy. Avarice once believed in My Provision, and trusted in My Faithfulness. However, as the fog started to settle over the valley, worry caused her to trust in wealth itself over the Source. Avarice is the least asleep of all the Jeweled Ones in Slumber, for she sees the emptiness of Law's and Doctrine's practices. Instead of coming to Me about her hurt and fears though, she allowed them to become bitterness and resentment. She strives for more, and uses what she has to manipulate Law, Doctrine, and others. And though she does see the brokenness of Slumber, and acknowledges the fog over the valley, she refuses to surrender to the Light. Her trust lies in her own provision and the fleeting security it gives her, and she does not want to lose hold of it."

Prism allowed the words of the Father to enter deeply into her heart, and hid them there.

"I tell you these things, child, so that you may have compassion for Law, Doctrine, and Avarice, even though they hurt and neglected you." The Father continued, "Only with compassion, and by being filled with the Love of Us, will you be able to awaken my children."

The Father wiped a tear from His face. "None of my children were created bad. They only are misguided, asleep, and unaware of the fullness of who they are and whose they are. They need to be awakened, to know Us and love Us again. For in a short while my Son will return to the valley to bring all my children, all those who truly loved Us, home. And My desire is that not one of my children are kept from coming home."

Prism took a deep breath. Even her breaths now felt they held the Father in them. "I will do my best, Father."

"We know you will." He replied as He gently placed her again on a cloud. Prism settled into the soft, cotton-candy air, unsure if she was ready to go back, but knowing that she must.

"One more thing," said the Father before He released her. "Let me reveal one more mystery to you. You are always welcome to walk the ancient path, Prism, no matter where you go. For there are many other valleys in my Kingdom that need awakening, just like Slumber. But know this, the ancient path, the Spirit Pool, is within you. You carry the gateway to Celestia inside you, just as you carry My Son and Spirit within you.

Remember this, for only by traveling that path and visiting with me will you maintain the clarity and purpose of your crown. Visit with Us, and let Us share more mysteries with you. Allow Me to polish your crown so that it, and you, may always be clear so that the Light will shine through you the living colors of revelation. Remember to always choose the greater thing, lest the fog over the valley begin to cover your eyes and you too start to fall asleep."

"Oh, I will!" Replied Prism, excited to know that she may always return to this wonderful place.

With a pinch of His finger, the Father picked up the tiny crown and gently placed it back on His daughter's head. Then He touched His finger to her heart.

"I give you My heart, so that you will always be guided by compassion for My children." He said.

The Son walked up to Prism and took her hands. "I give you My hands," said the Son, "to create beautiful things that touch others and gives them Life."

Lastly, Spirit floated over and twirled around the child, then placed a soft kiss on her forehead. "I give you My eyes," said Spirit, "so that you may always see the Work and Will of the Father, and that His many realms and mysteries may be revealed to you."

With that, the Father gently blew Prism and the cloud off again into the Light. As she started to leave Celestia and began to sink back through the Spirit Pool, she heard the Son call out: "And remember, that We are with you, until the end of the ages."

I started this story with a secret, that she was a Diamond. A Diamond among diamonds who forgot who they are. Just a child of the Great King Divine, she saw the wonder and beauty of His Spirit all around her. Her name was Prism, for she was created to allow His Light to fill her and shine through her.

Now sleeper, it's time to wake up.

"Lift up your heads, O you gates! And be lifted up, you everlasting doors! And the King of glory shall come in." Psalms 24:7 NKJV

"Then I heard the voice of the Lord, saying, 'Whom shall I send, and who will go for Us?' Then I said, 'Here am I. Send me!'" Isaiah 6:8 AMP

"As for me, because I am innocent, I will see Your face until I see You for who You really are. Then I will awaken with Your form, and be fully satisfied, fulfilled in the revelation of Your glory in me!"
Psalms 17:15 TPT

About the Author

Michaela Adeline Cozad, known as Michaela Adeline in her profession, is lover of Christ who works as an artist and arts teacher. In 2019, she felt the call to help others discover their creative authority, and with the blessing of her Pastor and leaders, started hosting small prophetic art classes in her home. Here recently, at the beginning of 2021, Michaela felt the Lord once again calling her to pursue some God-sized dreams. The first being to start a traveling prophetic art ministry "Lotus Crown Art Studio." The second was to share her spiritual journey and experiences with the Lord in a divinely inspired children's book, "Up the Ancient Pathway: A Children's Book for All Ages."

Michaela's prayer is that every person who reads this book will feel the tangible presence of Father. That they will be awakened by the light of His love, and will jump into the spirit-pool to visit Him as His precious children once again.

Heaven's Heart for Earth

Seraph Creative is a collective of artists, writers, theologians & illustrators who desire to see the body of Christ grow into full maturity, walking in their inheritance as Sons Of God on the Earth.

Sign up to our newsletter to know about future exciting releases.

Visit our website :

www.seraphcreative.org

Up the Ancient Pathway

Copyright© 2022 by Michaela Cozad

All rights reserved. This book is protected by the USA, UK and international copyright laws. This book may not be copied or reprinted for commercial gain or profit. The use of short quotations or occasional page copying for personal or group study is permitted and encouraged. Permission will be granted upon request.

Illustration by Michaela Cozad

Published by Seraph Creative in 2022
United States / United Kingdom / South Africa / Australia
www.seraphcreative.org

Layout & Typesetting: Feline Graphics
www.felinegraphics.com

Printed in USA, UK and RSA, 2022

All rights reserved. No part of this book, artwork included, may be used or reproduced in any matter without the written permission of the publisher.

ISBN 978-1-922428-50-9

Made in the USA
Coppell, TX
26 May 2022